Echoes of Your Name

Navigating the Mind's Loops with Awareness and Compassion

Shyamankar Singhari

Echoes of Your Name

This book is a work of nonfiction, created to provide insight, guidance, and reflection. While every effort has been made to ensure accuracy, the author and publisher make no warranties as to the completeness or applicability of the contents and shall not be held responsible for any damages arising from the use of this material.

Published by WKRISHIND
wkrishind.in

Author: Shyamankar Singhari
Publisher: WKRISHIND

First Edition, 2025

ISBN: 978-81-981954-2-5

Preface

In the quiet moments of our lives, a name, a memory, or a fleeting thought can surface, pulling us into a loop of emotions and questions. These echoes are not merely distractions; they are invitations to explore the depths of our minds and hearts. *Echoes of Your Name* is a guide for those who find themselves caught in the rhythm of recurring thoughts, offering practical tools, reflective exercises, and compassionate insights to transform these loops into opportunities for self-discovery.

This book emerged from my own experiences with mental loops—those uninvited thoughts that seemed to hold me captive until I learned to listen to them with curiosity rather than resistance. Through years of reflection, study, and practice, I discovered that these echoes carry messages about our desires, fears, and unresolved emotions. By sharing this journey, I hope to provide a roadmap for others to navigate their own echoes with grace and understanding.

Each chapter builds on the last, guiding you from acknowledging the first stirrings of a memory to cultivating a life of presence and emotional freedom. Whether you are grappling with nostalgia, longing, or uncertainty, this book offers a framework to observe, process, and release these thoughts without losing the love or lessons they hold.

May these pages serve as a gentle companion, helping you transform the weight of recurring thoughts into a lighter, more intentional way of living.

- Shyamankar Singhari

Author's Note

Writing *Echoes of Your Name* has been a deeply personal journey, rooted in my own encounters with the persistent thoughts that shape our emotional landscapes. This book is not a clinical manual or a one-size-fits-all solution. Instead, it is a heartfelt exploration of the human experience, blending mindfulness, journaling, visualization, and grounding techniques to help you navigate the echoes of your mind.

The exercises and reflections in these pages are designed to be flexible—adapt them to your needs, pace, and comfort. If a memory or emotion feels overwhelming, pause and return when ready. The goal is not to erase the past but to integrate it with compassion, allowing you to live more fully in the present.

I encourage you to approach this book with curiosity and patience. Your echoes are unique, and so is your path to understanding them. Thank you for inviting this work into your journey—I hope it brings you clarity, calm, and a deeper connection to yourself.

- Shyamankar Singhari

Dedication

To those who hear the whispers of the past and seek to understand their heart's quiet messages—may you find clarity, peace, and freedom in your journey.

Content

Part 1 — The Arrival of the Echo

Chapter 1:
The First Echo

It begins subtly. A name drifts into your mind, uninvited, almost like a whisper from the past. You're going about your day—walking, working, scrolling through your phone—and suddenly, there it is. The sound of it feels familiar, electric, yet unsettling. This is the first echo.

At first, it surprises you. "Why now?" you wonder. There is no apparent trigger—no photo, no message, no conversation. But your mind has a way of looping, of holding onto fragments of people who have left an impression on your heart. It doesn't ask for permission. It simply appears.

These initial echoes often feel like a mix of nostalgia and anxiety. You may catch yourself recalling tiny details: the tone of their voice, the curve of a smile, the way their laughter filled a room. And then comes the ripple effect—the memories that follow, each connected by invisible threads.

What is important to understand at this stage is that this is normal. Our minds are wired to remember emotionally significant experiences, especially ones tied to affection, curiosity, or unresolved feelings. The echo isn't a threat; it is a messenger, trying to tell you something about your emotions, your desires, or even your fears.

Rather than resisting it, notice it. Name it: *This is an echo.* Observe the emotions it stirs. Are you anxious, joyful, wistful? Awareness is the first step in transforming these recurring thoughts from a source of discomfort into a guide for self-understanding.

In the following chapters, we'll explore why these echoes appear, how they loop, and how you can navigate them without being consumed. For now, allow yourself the simple act of acknowledgment. The first echo is not a chain—it's an invitation to see your mind, your heart, and your memories with clarity and compassion.

Chapter 2:
The Mind's Replay

After the first echo arrives, the mind often begins its familiar ritual: replay. One thought sparks another, looping through memories, feelings, and "what ifs." This is not random—it's your brain's way of processing significance, especially when emotions are involved.

Imagine a song stuck in your head. A single note repeats, over and over, until your mind works through it. Memories of people function in much the same way. Each repetition is your mind's attempt to understand, predict, or make sense of emotional experiences. The mind seeks closure, comprehension, or sometimes just the comfort of familiarity.

This replay can feel overwhelming. You might notice yourself imagining scenarios, replaying conversations, or scrutinizing small gestures for hidden meaning. The loop can carry pleasure, pain, or both simultaneously. This duality—where warmth and anxiety coexist—is a hallmark of emotional replay.

The key to navigating these loops is awareness. Recognize when your mind is replaying:

- A phrase you said or heard.

- A glance or expression that lingered in memory.
- An imagined future interaction.

Instead of judging yourself for these thoughts, label them: *This is my mind replaying.* Observing without self-criticism reduces the emotional charge and allows you to see patterns.

In time, you'll learn that replay is not a trap. It is an opportunity—a signal that your mind is seeking understanding, emotional resolution, or insight into your desires. With gentle observation, you can move from being caught in the loop to engaging with it consciously, transforming each replay into a tool for self-awareness.

In the next chapter, we will explore how echoes appear not only in the mind but also in your surroundings, creating a web of reminders that feel both random and meaningful. Understanding this helps you step out of automatic reactions and approach each echo with clarity.

Chapter 3:
Shadows in the Surroundings

Once the mind begins its replay, the echoes often extend beyond thoughts and memories—they appear in the world around you. A song, a street, a smell, even a stranger's glance can spark recognition. These "shadows" in your surroundings act as subtle reminders, pulling the memory forward as if it never left.

It can feel uncanny. You might walk past a café and remember a conversation, or hear a fragment of a melody that instantly takes you back. Objects, places, or patterns of behavior become triggers, activating the loop again. The more significant the emotional attachment, the more sensitive your mind becomes to these external echoes.

Understanding this connection between mind and environment is crucial. Recognizing that a trigger is external—not a sign that something is "happening" now—helps you respond consciously rather than reactively. Pause and observe:

- **Notice:** What exactly triggered this memory?
- **Label:** This is a memory, not a prediction.

- **Anchor:** Focus on the present moment—your breath, surroundings, or body sensations.

These shadows can feel intrusive, but they are not inherently negative. They are opportunities to notice patterns, explore emotions, and practice grounding yourself in reality. By acknowledging their presence without judgment, you reclaim your mind from automatic loops.

In the next chapter, we will delve into **triggers and patterns** more deeply, helping you identify what sparks your mind's echoes and how to work with them instead of being overwhelmed.

Part 2 — Understanding the Loops

Chapter 4:

Triggers and Patterns

Our minds are intricate networks, linking memories, emotions, and sensory experiences. When a name, face, or memory keeps appearing, it's rarely random—there's usually a trigger, a spark that sets the loop in motion.

What is a trigger?

A trigger is anything—internal or external—that activates a memory or emotion. It could be a place, a sound, a word, a smell, or even a fleeting thought. For example:

- Hearing a song you once shared
- Passing a familiar street or café
- Seeing someone who reminds you of them
- A certain time of day or season

These triggers often follow **patterns**. Over time, you might notice that certain times, moods, or situations consistently bring the memory back. Perhaps late evenings are more intense, or moments of loneliness act as a magnet for recall. Observing these patterns is the first step to breaking the automatic loop.

Why patterns matter:
Understanding patterns helps you recognize that these recurring thoughts aren't arbitrary—they are conditioned responses. Once you identify what triggers them, you can:

- Anticipate moments of vulnerability
- Prepare grounding techniques in advance
- Slowly reduce the emotional charge linked to the memory

Practical exercise:

1. Take a small notebook and label it *Triggers & Patterns.*
2. Every time the memory or name resurfaces, note:
    - The trigger (internal or external)
    - Your emotional response
    - How long the thought persisted
3. Review weekly to identify repeating triggers and emotional patterns.

Awareness alone begins to shift your relationship with these loops. You move from feeling swept away to observing your mind's responses, gaining a sense of control.

In the next chapter, we will explore **Fear, Desire, and Curiosity**—how your emotions interact with these triggers and keep the mind looping even when logic says, "It's just a memory."

Chapter 5:
Fear, Desire, and Curiosity

Once we recognize the triggers and patterns of recurring thoughts, another layer emerges—our emotions. Fear, desire, and curiosity often intertwine, creating a cycle that keeps the memory alive.

Fear

Fear is one of the most powerful magnets for looping thoughts. It can manifest as:

- Fear of loss: "What if I never see them again?"
- Fear of betrayal or rejection: "What if they don't care?"
- Fear of missing out on connection or closure

Fear keeps the mind alert, replaying scenarios to protect us—even if those scenarios are unlikely. This protective instinct can, ironically, keep us stuck in loops rather than helping us move forward.

Desire

Desire fuels longing—the pull of wanting to see, hear, or feel that person again. Desire is not just about romantic attraction; it can be the craving for familiarity, comfort, or validation. The stronger the desire, the more the mind gravitates toward memories, imagining interactions, and replaying moments.

Curiosity

Curiosity acts like a silent conductor behind the scenes. Questions such as:

- "What are they doing now?"
- "Do they think about me?"
- "What if things had been different?"
  These "what if" scenarios amplify the mental loops, creating endless variations of reality that never fully exist.

Why these three are intertwined

Fear, desire, and curiosity form a triangular feedback loop. Fear triggers the mind to scan for potential threats or loss, desire heightens emotional intensity, and curiosity fills in gaps with imagined stories. Together, they sustain repetitive thinking, making it difficult to let go.

Practical exercise:

1. When a recurring thought arises, pause and ask yourself:

    - Am I experiencing fear?

    - Am I experiencing desire?
    - Am I experiencing curiosity or "what if" thinking?

2. Label the emotion without judgment. Simply note it in a journal: "This is fear" or "This is curiosity."

3. Take three deep breaths and remind yourself: It's okay to feel this, but it's not the full reality.

Observing your emotions instead of reacting to them gradually loosens the grip of recurring thoughts. By naming fear, desire, and curiosity, you reclaim part of the control the mind once held over you.

In the next chapter, we will explore **The Dance of Certainty and Doubt**—how trust, imagination, and past experiences create conflicting thoughts that intensify loops.

Chapter 6:

The Dance of Certainty and Doubt

By now, you may have noticed that recurring thoughts don't simply appear—they often swing between extremes. One moment, your mind is filled with certainty: "I know how they feel about me," or "I am sure this is how it happened." The next, doubt seeps in: "Maybe I misread everything," or "Perhaps they've forgotten me entirely." This push-and-pull creates a mental dance that can feel exhausting.

The Role of Certainty

Certainty gives the mind a sense of control. It tries to create a narrative that feels safe and predictable. When certainty takes hold, you may find yourself:

- Clinging to memories that "prove" your beliefs
- Replaying moments to confirm imagined patterns
- Seeking reassurance through imagined or real-world cues

Certainty can feel comforting, but it can also trap you in a loop. The brain often exaggerates patterns and connections to maintain its narrative, even if reality is more nuanced.

The Role of Doubt

Doubt, on the other hand, is the mind's reminder that it cannot know everything. Doubt surfaces as:

- Questioning your interpretation of past interactions
- Imagining alternative outcomes
- Wondering whether you are misremembering or overthinking

Doubt is not inherently bad—it prevents blind attachment—but when paired with certainty, it fuels mental oscillation. The swing between "I am sure" and "I have no idea" keeps your thoughts returning to the same person or memory again and again.

Why this dance occurs

The interplay of certainty and doubt often stems from three sources:

1. **Past experiences** – Memories of betrayal, abandonment, or confusion heighten both the need for certainty and the fear of being wrong.

2. **Attachment style** – People who deeply invest emotionally in others are more prone to oscillate between hope and fear.

3. **Imagination** – The mind naturally fills gaps in memory or understanding, creating scenarios that may never have existed.

Practical exercise:

1. When a thought swings between certainty and doubt, pause and name the swing: "This is certainty" or "This is doubt."

2. Ask yourself: What do I know for sure? What am I imagining?

3. Ground yourself in the present with a simple sensory check: notice five things you can see, four things you can touch, three things you can hear, two things you can smell, and one thing you can taste.

By recognizing the dance rather than being pulled into it, you create space to observe your mind rather than be consumed by it. Awareness of this swing is the first step toward mastering your thoughts instead of letting them master you.

In the next section, we will move into **Part 3 — Navigating the Echoes**, where practical strategies help reduce the intensity of recurring thoughts while fostering calm and clarity.

Part 3 — Navigating the Echoes

Chapter 7:

Observing Without Judgement

Recurring thoughts can feel like waves crashing over you—sometimes gentle, sometimes overwhelming. The natural instinct is to push them away, fight them, or chase answers. But the more you resist, the stronger they seem to become. This is where the practice of observing without judgement comes in.

What it means to observe

Observing without judgement is simply noticing your thoughts as they are, without labeling them "good" or "bad," "healthy" or "crazy." You allow the mind to express itself, while you remain the witness.

Think of it like watching clouds pass in the sky. Some are dark, some are bright, some are shaped like familiar things. You notice them, perhaps even admire them, but you do not try to control their movement.

Why judgement fuels loops

Every time you judge a thought, you add emotional weight to it. Saying to yourself, "Why do I keep thinking about them?" or "I shouldn't feel this way" amplifies anxiety and keeps the mental loop active. Judgement is a signal to the mind that something is wrong, which triggers more mental energy toward the same thoughts.

Techniques to practice observation

1. **Label your thoughts**: When a recurring thought arises, quietly name it. For example: "Here is a thought about their name" or "Here is a worry about what they might be doing."

2. **Notice your body's reaction**: Pay attention to tension in your chest, a racing heartbeat, or shallow breathing. Observing physical responses can help you separate emotion from thought.

3. **Breathe and return to the present**: Focus on your breath for a few cycles. With each exhale, imagine releasing some of the energy attached to the thought.

4. **Practice daily mindfulness**: Even five minutes a day of mindful observation—watching sounds, sensations, or your surroundings—strengthens the habit of observing without being swept away.

The power of non-reactivity

By observing without judgement, you reclaim choice. You are no longer at the mercy of each thought. Some thoughts may still recur, but you learn that noticing them does not require action, emotion, or obsession.

Practical exercise:

- Sit quietly for ten minutes. Close your eyes and observe your thoughts.
- Each time a recurring thought about them appears, silently note: "Thought appearing" and return to observing your breath.
- At the end, journal any insights—without judgment—about what patterns you noticed.

This chapter marks the beginning of a shift—from being trapped in mental loops to developing the ability to witness them. In the next chapter, we will explore **writing the loops away**, turning observation into a tangible tool for emotional release.

Chapter 8:
Writing the Loops Away

Observing your thoughts is the first step. The next is giving them a safe space to be expressed—on paper. Writing can transform the energy of repetitive thoughts into clarity, understanding, and even release.

Why writing works

The act of writing shifts thoughts from the abstract world of your mind into something tangible. When you see your thoughts on paper, you gain perspective. Loops that once felt endless begin to take shape as patterns, stories, or emotions that can be examined, understood, and gently released.

Getting started

1. **Choose your medium**: A journal, notebook, or digital document—whatever feels accessible and safe.

2. **Create a safe space**: Sit in a quiet place, free from distractions. A cup of tea or soft music can help set the tone.

3. **Start with free writing**: Don't censor or judge yourself. Write whatever comes to mind when your recurring thought arises.

    - Example: "Her name keeps appearing in my mind. I feel anxious, hopeful, confused... I don't know why I can't stop thinking about her."

4. **Notice patterns**: After a few sessions, read what you've written. Are there recurring fears, desires, or "what ifs"? Recognizing patterns helps you understand the loops instead of being trapped by them.

Transforming emotion into clarity

Writing isn't just about venting; it's a tool for reflection. Once the thought is on paper:

- **Ask questions**: "Why is this thought appearing?" "What am I afraid of?" "What do I really want?"

- **Respond from your present self**: Write answers as if you are comforting a friend or your own inner self. This builds compassion and perspective.

Exercises to release loops through writing

- **Dialogue with your thought**: Write a conversation between you and the recurring thought. Ask questions, express feelings, and allow the thought to respond.

- **Letter of release**: Write a letter addressed to the person or memory, acknowledging emotions and then gently letting go. You do not need to send it.

- **Tracking triggers**: Note the situations, words, or places that bring the thought back. Awareness is the first step toward reducing their power.

The power of repetition

Daily or frequent writing strengthens the habit. Even ten minutes a day can provide remarkable insights. Over time, what once felt like an uncontrollable mental loop becomes manageable, and the act of writing turns into a trusted ally.

Transition to next chapter

Once you've learned to observe and write your recurring thoughts, the next step is to anchor yourself in the present moment. In the following chapter, we will explore **mental anchors and grounding**, practical techniques to reconnect with reality and reduce the emotional pull of these loops.

Chapter 9:

Mental Anchors and Grounding

Writing down recurring thoughts helps you understand them, but understanding alone is not always enough. When a loop resurfaces, it can feel as though your mind has been swept away by a strong current. Mental anchors and grounding practices give you a way to pull yourself back to the present, regaining control and clarity.

What grounding is

Grounding is the process of connecting your awareness to the present moment. It stabilizes your thoughts and emotions, helping you observe recurring loops without being consumed by them. Think of it as planting your feet firmly on the ground when your mind starts to wander.

Simple grounding techniques

1. **Five Senses Exercise**

    - Look around and name **five things you can see**.
    - Identify four things you can touch.
    - Notice three things you can hear.

- Recognize two things you can smell.
- Focus on **one thing you can taste**. This brings your attention back to the immediate environment, reducing the intensity of mental loops.

2. **Breathing Anchor**

- Take slow, deep breaths: inhale for four counts, hold for four, exhale for four, pause for four.
- Focus solely on your breath. This rhythm becomes a mental anchor when thoughts feel overwhelming.

3. **Physical Connection**

- Press your feet against the floor, hands on your lap, or touch a textured object.
- Notice the sensation. Physical touch reminds your mind that you are grounded in reality.

4. **Name the Loop**

    - Give your recurring thought a simple label: “the echo,” “the worry,” or “the loop.”
    - Naming it creates distance and allows you to observe it objectively.

5. **Movement as Anchor**
    - Gentle stretching, walking, or yoga can reconnect your mind and body, offering a natural pause from intrusive thoughts.

Creating your personal anchoring toolkit

Experiment with these techniques and identify which ones feel most effective for you. You can even combine them: write your thought, breathe deeply, and then step outside for a few minutes, feeling the ground beneath your feet. The more consistently you practice, the easier it becomes to return to presence when loops arise.

Part 4 – Transforming the Echoes

Chapter 10:
Understanding the Emotional Messages

Recurring thoughts don't appear randomly—they carry messages from your heart and mind. When a name, memory, or image keeps surfacing, it often reflects deeper emotions, unmet needs, or unresolved questions. Understanding these messages allows you to respond consciously rather than react automatically.

Recognizing the signals

1. **Emotional intensity** - Notice how strongly you feel when a thought arises. Fear, longing, curiosity, or sadness can all reveal what matters to you most.

2. **Physical responses** - A racing heart, tight chest, or sudden tension in your body can indicate unresolved emotions tied to the thought.

3. **Recurring patterns** - Pay attention to which thoughts appear repeatedly. Are they linked to past heartbreak, insecurity, or a desire for closeness?

Why your mind repeats certain thoughts

- **Unmet needs** – Your mind may be signaling a need for connection, understanding, or validation that hasn't been fully addressed.

- **Attachment patterns** – Loops often reveal how you relate to others emotionally, showing where trust, fear, or dependency might linger.

- **Emotional processing** – Sometimes repetition is simply your brain's way of helping you process experiences you haven't fully accepted or understood.

Exercises for understanding the messages

1. **Ask "Why?"**

    - When a thought appears, write it down and ask: "Why does this affect me? What need or fear is underneath?"

2. **Dialogue with the thought**

    - Imagine having a conversation with the recurring thought. Ask it what it wants you to notice.

3. **Identify patterns across time**
    - Review past loops and see if common themes emerge. Patterns often reveal underlying emotional messages that require attention.

Turning insight into action

Understanding is not just about awareness—it's about responding constructively. Once you recognize what a recurring thought is signaling, you can address the need, adjust your behavior, or soothe your emotional response. This transforms loops from sources of distress into opportunities for self-awareness and growth.

Chapter 11:

Releasing Attachment, Keeping Love

Love and attachment are not the same. Often, the pain of recurring thoughts comes from clinging to someone, a memory, or a version of the past. True emotional freedom doesn't mean erasing love—it means releasing attachment while honoring the heart.

Understanding attachment vs. love

- **Attachment** ties your happiness to someone else's actions or presence. It can create anxiety, loops, and obsessive thinking.

- **Love** allows care, respect, and affection without dependency. It's about feeling connection while maintaining your inner stability.

Why attachment loops appear

Recurring thoughts often signal attachment. Your mind revisits memories or names because it fears loss, uncertainty, or disconnection. This isn't weakness—it's your heart asking for recognition, closure, or understanding.

Steps to release attachment while keeping love

1. **Acknowledge your emotions**
    - Don't fight what you feel. Write down your thoughts, name your feelings, and allow yourself to experience them fully.
2. **Separate the person from the memory**
    - Recognize that the love or connection you feel doesn't need to be tied to the present behavior or availability of someone else.
3. **Practice self-compassion**
    - Speak to yourself as you would to a friend. "It's okay to care deeply while letting go of what I cannot control."
4. **Shift from clinging to gratitude**
    - Reflect on the positive lessons, memories, or growth the relationship or memory has given you, instead of focusing on what you cannot have.
5. **Anchor in the present**

    - Each time a thought resurfaces, gently bring yourself back to the here and now. Notice your surroundings, your breath, or something grounding in your body.

Exercise: Heart vs. Loop

- When a name or memory appears repeatedly, write two columns: one for your **looping attachment thoughts** and one for your **heart's loving perspective**.

- Example:

    - Loop: "I can't stop thinking about them. I miss them. I need them to feel complete."

    - Heart: "I care for them and appreciate what we shared. I can feel love without needing them to be present."

Transition to next chapter
With attachment gently released, the mind becomes calmer, and love can exist without obsession. The next chapter, **Chapter 12 — The Power of Imagination and Safe Reflection**, explores how visualization and guided mental exercises can help process emotions constructively, turning recurring thoughts into opportunities for healing and growth.

Chapter 12:

The Power of Imagination and Safe Reflection

Our minds are powerful storytellers. When a name or memory loops repeatedly, imagination can either trap us in distress or guide us toward healing. Learning to use visualization safely allows you to process emotions without being consumed by them.

Why imagination matters

Recurring thoughts often replay scenarios that never happened, or exaggerate fears and doubts. This mental loop is the brain's way of trying to resolve uncertainty. Instead of resisting it, you can redirect imagination toward constructive reflection.

Safe reflection techniques

1. **Guided Visualization**
    - Close your eyes and picture a calm, safe space.
    - Invite the memory or the name to appear in a neutral or positive context.

- Observe emotions that arise without judgment. Let them come and go.

2. **Rewriting the Scene**

   - Mentally reimagine a moment with the person, but with a peaceful or healing outcome.

   - Example: If your mind replays tension or fear, imagine the same moment with calm understanding, compassion, or closure.

3. **Dialoguing with Your Mind**

   - Imagine having a conversation between your present self and the looping mind.

   - Your present self can reassure: "I see you, and it's safe. We are learning from this memory, not trapped by it."

4. **Creative Expression**

   - Sketch, journal, or narrate your mental scenes. Putting them on paper or speaking them aloud externalizes loops and creates distance.

Benefits of safe reflection

- Reduces anxiety caused by obsessive thinking.
- Strengthens your sense of agency and emotional resilience.
- Converts repetitive thoughts into insights about your needs, fears, and values.

Exercise: The Healing Scene

1. Close your eyes and recall a recurring memory.
2. Create a mental scene where the outcome is nurturing and safe.
3. Note any feelings or insights that arise.
4. Write them down to track progress over time.

Chapter 13:

Trusting Life and Higher Guidance

When thoughts loop repeatedly, the mind often feels like it's spiraling out of control. In these moments, trusting something larger than yourself—life, a higher power, or your own inner guidance—can provide a stabilizing anchor.

Why trust matters

Recurring thoughts thrive on uncertainty. When you doubt outcomes, question intentions, or fear the unknown, loops gain strength. Trust acts as a mental and emotional buffer, allowing you to observe thoughts without being swept away.

Ways to cultivate trust

1. **Faith in Life's Flow**
    - Recognize that not every detail of life is within your control.
    - Accepting uncertainty doesn't mean passivity—it means letting go of unnecessary suffering caused by trying to control everything.
2. **Spiritual Anchors**

- Prayer, meditation, or reflection can help quiet the mind.
- Even a few minutes of focused breathing while repeating a phrase like "I am safe, I am guided" can shift perspective.

3. **Inner Guidance**
    - Reflect on past experiences where you overcame fear or found solutions unexpectedly.
    - Write down moments where trusting yourself or circumstances led to positive outcomes. This reinforces confidence in your inner compass.

4. **Symbolic Rituals**
    - Light a candle, play calming music, or create a small daily ritual to signify letting go of obsessive thoughts.
    - Rituals give a tangible sense of release and reinforce faith in the process.

Benefits of trusting higher guidance

- Reduces anxiety tied to looping thoughts.
- Encourages a sense of safety and calm in uncertainty.
- Builds resilience, helping you respond rather than react to recurring mental patterns.

Exercise: Anchoring Trust

1. Close your eyes and take deep breaths.
2. Visualize placing your worries into a safe container or releasing them into the universe.
3. Repeat silently or aloud: "I trust life to guide me, and I trust myself to handle what comes."
4. Journal any feelings or insights that arise.

Chapter 14:

When the Echoes Fade Naturally

Recurring thoughts can feel relentless, as if your mind is stuck on repeat. Yet, over time, many of these echoes gradually lose their intensity. Understanding how and why this happens can provide hope and reassurance during moments of mental looping.

Why echoes fade

- **Time and perspective:** The more distance you create between yourself and a past event or person, the less emotional charge it carries.

- **Emotional processing:** Each time you observe, reflect, or journal about a thought, you reduce its grip. Processing feelings safely allows the mind to release them naturally.

- **Shifts in priorities:** Life keeps moving forward. New experiences, responsibilities, and connections gradually replace old loops with fresh focus.

Signs that echoes are diminishing

1. **Decreased frequency:** Thoughts appear less often, leaving longer gaps of mental calm.

2. **Reduced intensity:** Memories or names evoke milder emotions rather than overwhelming waves.

3. **Improved clarity:** You can think of a memory without being swept into a spiral of "what ifs."

4. **Increased present awareness:** You notice yourself engaging more fully in the current moment instead of dwelling in the past.

Supporting the natural fade

- **Mindfulness:** Notice thoughts without judgment. Acknowledge them and let them pass, like clouds drifting in the sky.

- **Journaling:** Capture recurring thoughts and the emotions they bring. Writing provides a safe outlet and often reveals patterns you can release.

- **Grounding exercises:** Physical activities, breathing techniques, or sensory focus can shift attention away from looping thoughts.

- **Compassion:** Treat yourself kindly. Repeated thoughts are a normal part of the healing process; self-criticism only strengthens them.

Exercise: Observing the Fade

1. Identify one recurring thought you notice frequently.

2. Rate its emotional intensity on a scale of 1–10.

3. Over a week, track each time it arises and how intense it feels.

4. Observe any decrease in frequency or emotional charge, acknowledging even small improvements.

Reflection

The fading of echoes isn't always linear. Some days may feel heavier than others, and that's normal. Trust in the gradual release. Your mind is capable of recalibrating, letting go, and returning to balance.

Chapter 15:

Moving Forward While Keeping Memories

Letting go doesn't mean erasing memories. In fact, moving forward while honoring what has shaped you allows for both healing and growth. Memories, when viewed with awareness and balance, can become tools rather than traps.

Integrating the past

- **Acceptance over suppression:** Accept memories for what they are—a part of your life story—without trying to push them away or judge them.

- **Learning from experiences:** Each recurring thought or emotional loop often carries insight about your needs, values, or boundaries.

- **Selective focus:** You can choose which memories to reflect on and which ones to allow to fade into the background.

Balancing remembrance and presence

1. **Reflect intentionally:** Set aside a specific time to recall past experiences with curiosity rather than obsession.

2. **Anchor in the present:** After reflection, return attention to your current surroundings, sensations, and actions.

3. **Celebrate growth:** Recognize how your experiences, even painful ones, have contributed to who you are today.

Strategies for moving forward

- **Create a memory ritual:** This can be as simple as writing a letter to yourself or keeping a journal of lessons learned.

- **Visualize a future self:** Picture who you want to be and how you want to feel, using memories as guidance rather than chains.

- **Engage in meaningful activities:** Invest energy in hobbies, relationships, or projects that bring joy and fulfillment.

Exercise: Memory Integration

1. Choose one recurring memory that often triggers emotional loops.

2. Write down what you learned from it and how it shaped you positively.

3. Visualize placing it in a "memory shelf," where it is acknowledged but not allowed to control your daily thoughts.

4. End with a deep breath, grounding yourself in the present moment.

Reflection

Memories are neither enemies nor prisons—they are chapters in your story. By acknowledging them with compassion and learning from them, you can move forward without guilt, regret, or obsession.

Chapter 16:

Designing a Mindset of Presence

Living fully in the present is not about forgetting the past or ignoring the future. It's about consciously choosing where you place your attention and energy, moment by moment. A mindset of presence allows recurring thoughts to exist without dominating your mind.

Understanding presence

- **Awareness over autopilot:** Notice your thoughts, feelings, and surroundings without judgment.

- **Choice over reaction:** Presence gives you the space to respond intentionally rather than being swept away by loops or triggers.

- **Mindful engagement:** When fully immersed in your current experience, past echoes lose their power.

Practical strategies to cultivate presence

1. **Mindful breathing:**
   Focus on your breath for a few minutes each day. When thoughts of the past

arise, gently return your attention to the inhale and exhale.

2. **Sensory anchoring:**
   Notice five things you can see, four things you can touch, three things you can hear, two things you can smell, and one thing you can taste. This grounds you in the present.

3. **Intentional pauses:**
   Before responding to situations or making decisions, pause and check in with your body, thoughts, and emotions.

4. **Daily reflections:**
   End your day by noting one moment you fully experienced and one lesson you learned. This reinforces a habit of mindful presence.

Integrating past, present, and future

- **Acknowledge memories without dwelling:** Recognize past echoes as part of your story but return attention to the current moment.

- **Set future intentions without anxiety:** Use lessons from past experiences to make conscious choices for the future rather than being controlled by fear.

- **Celebrate small victories:** Every moment you redirect your focus to presence is a step toward mental freedom.

Exercise: Presence Practice

1. Set a timer for 5–10 minutes.
2. Sit comfortably, eyes closed, and focus on your breath.
3. When past memories or loops arise, gently name them ("thinking" or "remembering") and return to your breath.
4. Reflect briefly on how the exercise felt.

Reflection

Presence is a skill, not a destination. The more you practice, the less power your recurring thoughts have over you, and the more your mind becomes a space of calm, clarity, and choice.

Part 5 — Tools and Exercises

Chapter 17:

Journaling Prompts for Releasing Loops

Journaling is a powerful tool to explore recurring thoughts and release their emotional charge. Writing transforms abstract worries into concrete words, allowing you to examine, understand, and gently let go.

Why journaling helps

- Creates a safe space for reflection.
- Helps identify patterns and triggers.
- Allows the mind to process emotions without being trapped in loops.
- Shifts energy from rumination to conscious exploration.

How to journal effectively

1. **Set aside dedicated time:** Even 10–15 minutes daily can make a difference.
2. **Choose a quiet space:** Minimize distractions and allow yourself to focus inward.

3. **Write without judgment:** Don't worry about grammar, style, or length. Let your thoughts flow freely.

4. **Be honest:** Speak to yourself with compassion and clarity.

Sample prompts to release loops

1. *"Write the first memory that comes to mind when you hear their name. Then write a compassionate response from your present self."*

2. *"List three times when your mind looped on this person today. What triggered the thought each time?"*

3. *"Write a letter to your past self from today's perspective. What advice or comfort would you give?"*

4. *"Describe a scenario where you feel at peace and free from loops. What does it look like, feel like, and sound like?"*

5. *"Write down a fear about the future related to this person. Then write a rational and compassionate response that eases that fear."*

Journaling tips

- Use separate sections or notebooks for different prompts.
- Revisit older entries periodically to notice patterns and growth.
- If emotions become overwhelming, pause and return later. Pair journaling with grounding techniques.

Reflection

Journaling is not about forcing the mind to forget or suppress memories. It's about giving your thoughts a safe outlet, observing them with curiosity, and slowly loosening their grip. The more you practice, the lighter the echoes become.

Chapter 18:

Guided Visualization: Meeting Your Mind's Echo

Visualization is a gentle and safe way to meet the recurring thoughts or "echoes" that visit your mind. Unlike suppressing or avoiding them, guided visualization allows you to face these echoes with curiosity and compassion, transforming their emotional intensity.

Why visualization works

- Creates a safe mental space to explore emotions.
- Helps separate reality from imagination.
- Encourages understanding instead of fear or avoidance.
- Builds resilience and emotional clarity.

Preparing for your visualization

1. **Find a quiet space:** Sit or lie down comfortably.
2. **Close your eyes and breathe:** Take slow, deep breaths, letting your body relax.

3. **Set an intention:** Remind yourself that this practice is for understanding and healing.

Step-by-step guided visualization

1. **Visualize a calm place:** Imagine a serene location—a garden, beach, or quiet room—where you feel safe.

2. **Invite your echo:** Picture the name, face, or memory gently appearing in this space.

3. **Observe without judgment:** Notice the emotions, sensations, or thoughts that arise. Label them if helpful—"curiosity," "longing," "fear," "hope."

4. **Respond with compassion:** Imagine speaking to the echo kindly. For example, "I see you. I understand why you are here, but I am safe in the present."

5. **Integrate your present self:** Visualize yourself taking the echo's hand and guiding it into the calm space, transforming the intensity into a peaceful energy.

6. **Return to the present:** Gradually bring your attention back to your breath, your

body, and the room around you. Open your eyes when ready.

Tips for effective practice

- Start with 5–10 minutes, then gradually extend if comfortable.
- Repeat as needed, especially when loops feel strong.
- Keep a journal nearby to note insights, emotions, or patterns.
- Combine with grounding exercises like touching an object, walking, or stretching afterward.

Reflection

Meeting your mind's echo doesn't mean giving it control. It means acknowledging its presence, learning from it, and creating a safe mental space where you are in charge. Over time, the echoes will lose their intensity, and you'll feel more grounded and present.

Chapter 19:

Grounding Practices for Daily Life

Recurring thoughts and mental loops can feel overwhelming, especially when they intrude during daily activities. Grounding practices are practical strategies that help you reconnect with the present, stabilize your mind, and regain control over your thoughts.

Why grounding matters

- Reduces anxiety and overthinking.
- Prevents mental loops from escalating.
- Enhances emotional regulation.
- Connects you with your body and the present moment.

Simple grounding techniques

1. **The 5-4-3-2-1 Method**
   Engage your senses to anchor yourself:
    - 5 things you can see
    - 4 things you can touch
    - 3 things you can hear
    - 2 things you can smell

    - 1 thing you can taste

2. **Breathing Exercises**
    - **Box breathing:** Inhale for 4 counts, hold 4, exhale 4, hold 4.
    - **Counting breaths:** Count each breath up to 10, then start again. Focus brings the mind back from looping thoughts.

3. **Physical Connection**
    - Stretch, walk, or run.
    - Notice your feet touching the ground or your hands on an object.
    - Moving your body reestablishes a sense of presence and reality.

4. **Mindful Observation**
    - Choose an object or a small area in your surroundings.
    - Observe it in detail—the texture, color, shadows, patterns.
    - This redirects attention from mental loops to tangible reality.

5. **Journaling Breaks**

    - Write down the recurring thought without judgment.
    - Note emotions, triggers, and any new insights.
    - End with a grounding statement: "I *acknowledge this thought, and I return to now.*"

Integrating grounding into daily life

- Schedule mini grounding sessions throughout the day, even if loops aren't active.
- Combine techniques, e.g., breathing while walking, observing while journaling.
- Keep small reminders, like a stone in your pocket or a sticky note, to prompt grounding moments.

Reflection

Grounding is not about avoiding thoughts; it's about taking control over how they affect you. When practiced consistently, grounding helps you move from being a passive observer of mental loops to an active participant in your own emotional well-being.

Chapter 20:
Building Emotional Boundaries

Recurring thoughts can feel invasive, often blurring the line between reflection and obsession. Emotional boundaries are the tools that help protect your heart and mind without shutting down feelings or denying experiences.

Why boundaries matter

- They prevent mental exhaustion from overthinking.
- They allow you to feel without being overwhelmed.
- They create a safe space for healthy connections with yourself and others.
- They foster clarity and self-respect.

Steps to build emotional boundaries

1. **Recognize your limits**
    - Pay attention to when thoughts, emotions, or interactions become draining.
    - Note physical or emotional signals of discomfort -tension, anxiety, irritability.

2. **Name your feelings and triggers**

    - Identify the recurring thoughts or situations that provoke intense emotions.
    - Example: hearing a certain name triggers a loop of "what if" thoughts.
    - Acknowledgment is the first step in creating separation.

3. **Create safe mental spaces**

    - Visualize a protective boundary around your mind and heart.
    - Imagine you can observe thoughts without letting them control you.
    - Use phrases like: "I notice this thought, but I am not consumed by it."

4. **Communicate boundaries with others (if needed)**

    - Set limits on conversations or topics that provoke mental loops.
    - Politely redirect discussions if they cause undue emotional strain.

5. **Practice selective engagement**

    ○ Choose when and how deeply to engage with emotions, memories, or external stimuli.

    ○ Avoid forcing closure or resolution —let reflection happen naturally.

6. **Reinforce boundaries daily**

    ○ Grounding exercises, journaling, and mindfulness help maintain boundaries.

    ○ Remind yourself that protecting your mental space is an act of self-respect, not avoidance.

Reflection

Building emotional boundaries is not about shutting out love, memories, or thoughts. It's about gaining the ability to engage with your inner world consciously, without letting it dominate your present. Boundaries empower you to interact with life from a place of strength, not fear.

Chapter 21:

Trusting Life and Others Again

After building emotional boundaries, the next step is learning to trust—yourself, life, and the people around you. Trust is not blind; it is a conscious choice to engage with the world while honoring your past experiences and your emotional safety.

Why trust matters

- Trust allows meaningful connections without constant fear or doubt.
- It enables emotional growth and resilience.
- It prevents recurring thoughts from dominating your interactions and decisions.

Steps to cultivate trust

1. **Start with self-trust**
    - Acknowledge your ability to handle challenges and emotions.
    - Reflect on past experiences where you successfully navigated difficulties.

- Journaling prompt: "List three situations where I trusted myself and things worked out. How did I feel afterward?"

2. **Practice gradual exposure**
   - Start trusting life through small, manageable steps—letting go of minor worries, taking calculated risks, or trying new experiences.
   - Notice your responses and learn from them.

3. **Observe without assuming**
   - Avoid projecting fears or past patterns onto current situations or people.
   - Recognize that each person and circumstance is unique.

4. **Set boundaries while trusting**
   - Trust does not mean abandoning emotional boundaries.
   - Clear boundaries provide safety while still allowing vulnerability.

5. **Engage in reflective gratitude**

- Notice moments of positive outcomes, supportive relationships, or small coincidences that bring reassurance.
- Gratitude reinforces trust and creates mental habits that counter fear loops.

6. **Release the need for total certainty**
    - Accept that uncertainty is a part of life.
    - Trust is not about controlling outcomes but about approaching life with confidence in your resilience.

Reflection

Trust is a practice, not a guarantee. By trusting yourself and life, you open the door to genuine experiences and relationships while keeping your emotional space intact. Trusting others safely is a skill you build over time—it does not negate past pain but honors your capacity to move forward.

Chapter 22:

Reflection and Gratitude

As you move through the journey of noticing, understanding, and transforming recurring thoughts, taking time to reflect and practice gratitude becomes essential. Reflection allows you to see your progress, while gratitude anchors you in the present, reducing the power of mental loops.

Why reflection matters

- It helps you recognize patterns, triggers, and growth points.
- It allows you to honor the effort you've put into healing.
- It reinforces self-awareness, making it easier to maintain emotional balance.

Steps for meaningful reflection

1. **Review your journey**
    - Go back through your journal, exercises, or notes.
    - Observe the changes in your thoughts, reactions, and emotions over timc.

- Note moments when you handled loops with awareness rather than being consumed by them.

2. **Celebrate small victories**

    - Recognize each step forward, no matter how small.

    - Celebrate instances where you practiced trust, boundaries, or mindfulness successfully.

3. **Identify lessons learned**

    - Reflect on what recurring thoughts revealed about your desires, fears, and attachment patterns.

    - Ask yourself: "*What have I discovered about myself through this process?*"

Practicing gratitude

1. **Daily gratitude ritual**

    - Write down three things you are grateful for each day—experiences, people, or personal strengths.

    - Even noticing small positive moments strengthens your focus on the present.

2. **Gratitude for challenges**
    - Reflect on difficulties and loops not as burdens but as teachers.
    - Acknowledge the resilience you've cultivated by navigating them.
3. **Express gratitude outwardly**
    - Thank people who support or inspire you.
    - Small acts of appreciation create positive emotional connections and reinforce trust.

Reflection exercise

- Find a quiet space. Close your eyes and visualize your journey from the first echo to your present self.
- Notice the growth, the lessons, and the strength you've gained.
- Silently say: "I honor my journey. I am grateful for every step."

Chapter 23:

Moving Forward with Presence

After exploring the echoes of your mind, understanding the patterns, and practicing strategies to manage recurring thoughts, the final step is learning to live fully in the present. Presence is the bridge between reflection, growth, and freedom. It is where your mind stops looping and your life begins unfolding.

Why presence matters

- It allows you to experience life without being trapped in mental repetitions.
- It helps you engage authentically with yourself and others.
- It builds resilience, emotional stability, and joy.

Cultivating presence

1. **Mindful Awareness**
    - Pay attention to your senses: what you see, hear, feel, taste, and smell in each moment.
    - When an echo or loop arises, notice it without judgment and gently return to the present.

2. **Breathing as an Anchor**

    - Use deep, slow breaths to center yourself whenever your mind starts to wander.
    - A simple pattern: inhale for four counts, hold for four, exhale for four, pause for four.

3. **Engaging Fully in Activities**

    - Whether walking, eating, or talking with someone, immerse yourself in the experience.
    - Avoid multitasking and mental "replays." Presence grows with focused attention.

4. **Setting Intentions**

    - Each morning, remind yourself: "I choose presence today. I honor the moment I am in."
    - Intentions help guide your actions and reduce compulsive thinking.

Integrating lessons from the journey

- Recall the insights from observing loops, journaling, grounding, and guided visualizations.

- Recognize that your mind may still occasionally echo past thoughts, but you now have the tools to respond consciously.
- Embrace self-compassion when old patterns arise, knowing each moment of awareness strengthens your freedom.

Creating a life of emotional freedom

- Cultivate relationships and experiences that align with your values and joy.
- Practice gratitude, reflection, and mindfulness daily to keep the mind balanced.
- Trust that you can honor memories without being consumed by them.

Closing thought

Moving forward with presence is not about erasing the past—it's about engaging fully with life right now. It's the ultimate freedom: to live, to love, and to experience without the weight of recurring mental loops. Your journey from echoes to clarity has prepared you to step confidently into this new chapter of your life.

Printed at Repro India Ltd.